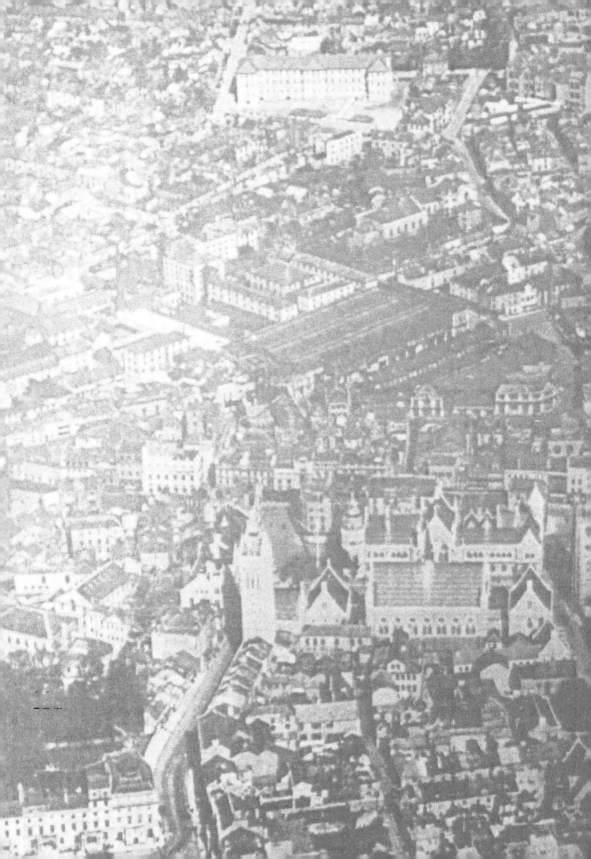

A CENTURY *of*
PLYMOUTH

Pictures of the lovely new Queen were everywhere, including the front windows of homes, and the Union flag often fluttered alongside. People everywhere looked forward to a bright new Elizabethan age. And it never happened!

A CENTURY *of*
PLYMOUTH

GUY FLEMING

The
History
Press

This book was first published in 2000 by Sutton Publishing Limited.

This new paperback edition first published in 2007 by Sutton Publishing

Reprinted in 2011 by
The History Press
The Mill, Brimscombe Mill,
Stroud, Gloucestershire, GL5 2QG
www.thehistorypress.co.uk

British Library Cataloguing in Publication Data
A catalogue record for this book is available from the British Library.

ISBN 978-0-7509-4898-2

Front endpaper: Plymouth before the outbreak of the Second World War.
Back endpaper: Plymouth Hoe, late 1990s.
Half title page: She may look a little fierce, with her determined face topped by a gold-rimmed pince-nez, but, then, Constance Hewitt was a battler for women's rights in her adopted city of Plymouth during the 1920s and '30s. She was the force behind the formation of what would now be called professional businesswomen's groups and fought discrimination against female workers.
Title page: Two bridges spanning the same river, joining Plymouth with Cornwall. The first, designed by Isambard Kingdom Brunel, was erected in 1859 and is still going strong. The second, a road bridge, was opened in 1962 by Queen Elizabeth, the Queen Mother.

Typeset in 11/14pt Photina.
Typesetting and origination by
Sutton Publishing.
Printed and bound in Great Britain by
Marston Book Services Limited, Didcot

Everything in the garden is lovely at Plymouth . . . This card seems evocative of a less frantic, more tranquil time when falling in love was a much slower and more tentative affair.

Contents

Protestors marched from all directions to make their feelings about the Poll Tax known in 1989 – and didn't the media revel in it all! You can see the effect on traffic as these marchers surged up one of the carriageways of Royal Parade. Most car drivers took it all in their stride.

Britain: A Century
of Change

Two women encumbered with gas masks go about their daily tasks during the early days of the war. (*Hulton Getty Picture Collection*)

The sixty years ending in 1900 were a period of huge transformation for Britain. Railway stations, post-and-telegraph offices, police and fire stations, gasworks and gasometers, new livestock markets and covered markets, schools, churches, football grounds, hospitals and asylums, water pumping stations and sewerage plants totally altered the urban scene, and the country's population tripled with more than seven out of ten people being born in or moving to the towns. The century that followed, leading up to the Millennium's end in 2000, was to be a period of even greater change.

When Queen Victoria died in 1901, she was measured for her coffin by her grandson Kaiser Wilhelm, the London prostitutes put on black mourning and the blinds came down in the villas and terraces spreading out from the old town centres. These centres were reachable by train and tram, by the new bicycles and still newer motor cars, were connected by the new telephone, and lit by gas or even electricity. The shops may have been full of British-made cotton and woollen clothing but the grocers and butchers were selling cheap Danish bacon, Argentinian beef, Australasian mutton and tinned or dried fish and fruit from Canada, California and South Africa. Most of these goods were carried in British-built-and-crewed ships burning Welsh steam coal.

As the first decade moved on, the Open Spaces Act meant more parks, bowling greens and cricket pitches. The First World War transformed the place of women, as they took over many men's jobs. Its other legacies were the war memorials which joined the statues of Victorian worthies in main squares round the land. After 1918 death duties and higher taxation bit hard, and a quarter of England changed hands in the space of only a few years.

The multiple shop – the chain store – appeared in the high street: Sainsburys, Maypole, Lipton's, Home & Colonial, the Fifty Shilling Tailor, Burton, Boots, W.H. Smith. The shopper was spoilt for choice, attracted by the brash fascias and advertising hoardings for national brands like Bovril, Pears Soap, and Ovaltine. Many new buildings began to be seen, such as garages, motor showrooms, picture palaces (cinemas), 'palais de dance', and ribbons of 'semis' stretched along the roads and new bypasses and onto the new estates nudging the green belts.

During the 1920s cars became more reliable and sophisticated as well as commonplace, with developments like the electric self-starter making them easier for women to drive. Who wanted to turn a crank handle in the new short skirt? This was, indeed, the electric age as much as the motor era. Trolley buses, electric trams and trains extended mass transport and electric light replaced gas in the street and the home, which itself was groomed by the vacuum cleaner.

A major jolt to the march onward and upward was administered by the Great Depression of the early 1930s. The older British industries

– textiles, shipbuilding, iron, steel, coal – were already under pressure from foreign competition when this worldwide slump arrived. Luckily there were new diversions to alleviate the misery. The 'talkies' arrived in the cinemas; more and more radios and gramophones were to be found in people's homes; there were new women's magazines, with fashion, cookery tips and problem pages; football pools; the flying feats of women pilots like Amy Johnson; the Loch Ness Monster; cheap chocolate and the drama of Edward VIII's abdication.

Things were looking up again by 1936 and new light industry was booming in the Home Counties as factories struggled to keep up with the demand for radios, radiograms, cars and electronic goods, including the first television sets. The threat from Hitler's Germany meant rearmament, particularly of the airforce, which stimulated aircraft and aero engine firms. If you were lucky and lived in the south, there was good money to be earned. A semi-detached house cost £450, a Morris Cowley £150. People may have smoked like chimneys but life expectancy, since 1918, was up by 15 years while the birth rate had almost halved.

In some ways it is the little memories that seem to linger longest from the Second World War: the kerbs painted white to show up in the blackout, the rattle of ack-ack shrapnel on roof tiles, sparrows killed by bomb blast. The biggest damage, apart from London, was in the south-west (Plymouth, Bristol) and the Midlands (Coventry, Birmingham).

A W.H.Smith shop front in Beaconsfield, 1922.

Postwar reconstruction was rooted in the Beveridge Report which set out the expectations for the Welfare State. This, together with the nationalisation of the Bank of England, coal, gas, electricity and the railways, formed the programme of the Labour government in 1945.

Times were hard in the late 1940s, with rationing even more stringent than during the war. Yet this was, as has been said, 'an innocent and well-behaved era'. The first let-up came in 1951 with the Festival of Britain and there was another fillip in 1953 from the Coronation, which incidentally

gave a huge boost to the spread of TV. By 1954 leisure motoring had been resumed but the Comet – Britain's best hope for taking on the American aviation industry – suffered a series of mysterious crashes. The Suez debacle of 1956 was followed by an acceleration in the withdrawal from Empire, which had begun in 1947 with the Independence of India. Consumerism was truly born with the advent of commercial TV and most homes soon boasted washing machines, fridges, electric irons and fires.

Children collecting aluminium to help the war effort, London, 1940s. (*IWM*)

The *Lady Chatterley* obscenity trial in 1960 was something of a straw in the wind for what was to follow in that decade. A collective loss of inhibition seemed to sweep the land, as the Beatles and the Rolling Stones transformed popular music, and retailing, cinema and the theatre were revolutionised. Designers, hairdressers, photographers

A street party to celebrate the Queen's Coronation, June 1953. (*Hulton Getty Picture Collection*)

and models moved into places vacated by an Establishment put to flight by the new breed of satirists spawned by *Beyond the Fringe* and *Private Eye*.

In the 1970s Britain seems to have suffered a prolonged hangover after the excesses of the previous decade. Ulster, inflation and union troubles were not made up for by entry into the EEC, North Sea Oil, Women's Lib or, indeed, Punk Rock. Mrs Thatcher applied the corrective in the 1980s, as the country moved more and more from its old manufacturing base over to providing services, consulting, advertising, and expertise in the 'invisible' market of high finance or in IT.

The post-1945 townscape has seen changes to match those in the worlds of work, entertainment and politics. In 1952 the Clean Air Act served notice on smogs and pea-souper fogs, smuts and blackened buildings, forcing people to stop burning coal and go over to smokeless sources of heat and energy. In the same decade some of the best urban building took place in the 'new towns' like Basildon, Crawley, Stevenage and Harlow. Elsewhere open warfare was declared on slums and what was labelled inadequate, cramped, back-to-back, two-up, two-down, housing. The new 'machine for living in' was a flat in a high-rise block. The architects and planners who promoted these were in league with the traffic engineers, determined to keep the motor car moving whatever the price in multi-storey car parks, meters, traffic wardens and ring roads. The old pollutant, coal smoke, was replaced by petrol and diesel exhaust, and traffic noise.

Punk rockers demonstrate their anarchic style during the 1970s. (*Barnaby's Picture Library*)

Fast food was no longer only a pork pie in a pub or fish-and-chips. There were Indian curry houses, Chinese take-aways and American-style hamburgers, while the drinker could get away from beer in a wine bar. Under the impact of television the big Gaumonts and Odeons closed or were rebuilt as multi-screen cinemas, while the palais de dance gave way to discos and clubs.

From the late 1960s the introduction of listed buildings and conservation areas, together with the growth of preservation societies, put a brake on 'comprehensive redevelopment'. The end of the century and the start of the Third Millennium see new challenges to the health of towns and the wellbeing of the nine out of ten people who now live urban lives. The fight is on to prevent town centres from dying, as patterns of housing and shopping change, and edge-of-town supermarkets exercise the attractions of one-stop shopping. But as banks and department stores close, following the haberdashers, greengrocers, butchers and ironmongers, there are signs of new growth such as farmers' markets, and corner stores acting as pick-up points where customers collect shopping ordered on-line from web sites.

Millennium celebrations over
the Thames at Westminster,
New Year's Eve, 1999.
(*Barnaby's Picture Library*)

Futurologists tell us that we are in stage two of the consumer revolu-
tion: a shift from mass consumption to mass customisation driven by
a desire to have things that fit us and our particular lifestyle exactly,
and for better service. This must offer hope for small city-centre shop
premises, as must the continued attraction of physical shopping,
browsing and being part of a crowd: in a word, 'shoppertainment'.
Another hopeful trend for towns is the growth in the number of young
people postponing marriage and looking to live independently, alone,
where there is a buzz, in 'swinging single cities'. Theirs is a 'flats-and-
cafés' lifestyle, in contrast to the 'family suburbs', and certainly fits in
with government's aim of building 60 per cent of the huge amount of
new housing needed on 'brown' sites, recycled urban land. There looks
to be plenty of life in the British town yet.

Plymouth: An Introduction

Plymouth can trace its maritime history back to 1000 BC when a Phoenician trading post, perhaps Britain's first commercial port, was established in Mount Batten, in Plymouth Sound.

In the 300 years after the Norman Conquest, Plymouth became the fourth largest town in England and one of the country's most important ports. The population of 7,000 was exceeded only by London, Bristol and York. It sent Members of Parliament from 1298 and was the first municipal corporation to be established by an Act of Parliament, in 1439.

In the early Middle Ages Plymouth's merchants and fishermen exported fish to France and imported salt and wine. In succeeding years exports to France, Spain, Portugal, the Mediterranean, the Netherlands and elsewhere, including the Americas, included not only fish but tin, woollen goods and lead, while imports ranged from wine, fruit and sugar to paper, hops and rye. The French, just across the Channel in Brittany, eyed all this with envy: they were responsible for sporadic raids from 1339 onwards. For instance, an invasion in 1403 saw thirty ships and 1,200 soldiers sailing into the Cattewater. The raiding party set 600 houses ablaze – hence the name given to that area, Bretonside. This impudent, daring incursion set the alarm bells ringing in London, and Henry V ordered a strengthening of defences. As a result, a castle was built to command the entrance to Sutton Harbour.

Plymouth's growing strategic importance as a naval centre had been recognised by Edward I in the thirteenth century when he brought England's first national navy together there – 325 ships of the line. This marked the genesis of an unrivalled cavalcade of ships, naval and mercantile, which were to set out from Plymouth to travel across the world, as, to a certain extent, they still do. Among the most glittering displays in Plymouth Sound must have been the Black Prince's huge fleet and army returned from crushing the French at Poitiers in 1357. The names of those who made their epic voyages of discovery from Plymouth read like a roll-call of Elizabethan nautical honour: Sir Richard Hawkins and his son, Sir John, who opened up the South Seas and the West Indies; John Oxenham, a Plymothian who became the first Englishman to

Diamond Jubilee Day, 1897. It must have seemed that Queen Victoria had been on the throne forever. She still had a few years to go. This is the scene on the Hoe at that time. Similar scenes are pending to celebrate the fiftieth anniversary of our present Queen's accession to the throne.

sail the Pacific Ocean to Mexico; Sir Humphrey Gilbert who took the first European settlers to North America and later sailed for Newfoundland; Sir Walter Raleigh, explorer, historian and victim of political intrigue; Sir Richard Grenville, who died fighting a Spanish fleet with one ship, the *Revenge*; Sir Martin Frobisher, who pioneered the exploration of the North-West Passage; Thomas Cavendish who became the second English sea captain – Sir Francis Drake was the first, in 1580 – to circumnavigate the globe. Many years later, in 1776, Captain James Cook sailed from Plymouth on his third voyage around the world. Drake, of course, is inescapably linked to Plymouth, from where he set sail to beat the Spanish Armada in 1588. He also made many private expeditions, which so ingratiated him with the Virgin Queen.

The voyage of the Pilgrim Fathers to Massachusetts in 1620 has also been woven into the colourful and varied tapestry of Plymouth's history. A little over twenty years later Plymouth was to go through one of its worst trials: from 1642 to 1646 it became a strategic cockpit of the Civil War. It spent three years under siege. Over 3,000 of the townsfolk died during this time and others faced starvation, as they held out against the Royalists. Three major attacks were repulsed, the most important victory being the so-called Sabbath Day fight, when the Cavaliers were flung back from Freedom Fields into Lipson Valley, where many drowned.

Puritan teaching and practice 'took on' to a great extent in Plymouth and it was no surprise when the town became the first municipality to declare for William of Orange when he landed in nearby Torbay in 1688.

The year 1691 was auspicious for the town because it marked the beginning of the dockyard, which was to exercise such a tremendous influence over a wide swathe of the south-west in coming decades. The first huts were built at the bottom of Cornwall Street and soon the vast tracts of meadowland and country estate adjoining it were swallowed by the development. Within 100 years the dockyard had established itself as one of the world's foremost naval arsenals, not least because of the incessant wars with France. Then the Crimean War in the early 1850s saw the dockyard seething with business while the Boer War, at the end of the century, made a deeper and more lasting impression because almost all of the thousands of troops in the garrison left for South Africa immediately. The dockyard's workforce went up to 20,000 in the First World War; it is still the biggest naval base in Western Europe.

Plymouth was very much a place of three towns – Plymouth, Devonport and Stonehouse – before the 'shot-gun marriage' of 1914 which saw the three hurriedly joined into one borough. Yet for twenty-five years after amalgamation its central shopping area remained largely as it had been during the previous century, built for the horse-drawn traffic and tramcar era.

One of the greatest sea processions of all time took place in October 1914 when an armada of thirty-three liners brought 25,000 troops from Canada. They had been bound for Southampton but were diverted to Plymouth because of a lurking submarine menace.

Plymouth's liner traffic grew greatly through the first part of the twentieth century, with over 788 vessels a year calling and disembarking passengers at the peak of activity. They included such luxury ships as the *Normandie*, *Liberté*, *Mauretania*, the *Bremen* and even Cunard's *Queen Mary*. Eventually, Southampton won through and the traffic slipped from Plymouth's grasp. Lloyd's listed Plymouth as closed to liner traffic in 1963.

Landing the catch at the fish market on the Barbican in its heyday, before 1900.

15

The dockyard suffered drastically during Service cut-backs of the 1920s and '30s, but rose to eminence again during the Second World War, when it achieved an enviable reputation for quick 'turnarounds' of stricken ships. The homecoming of HMS *Amethyst* from its engagagement with the Chinese in the Yangste in 1949 was another epic affair, as was Sir Francis Chichester's return from his around-the-world voyage in 1967.

The Blitz and subsequent rebuilding, featured in the Second World War and Beyond chapter, were catalysts for great change, forced and voluntary. Significant rebuilding programmes followed the bombing and changed the face of the city. Change has gathered pace again in the last decade, and still continues. Plymouth's marine leisure industry is growing quickly; Europe's largest production boat-building company has vital facilities in the city – Marine Projects enjoys a turnover of about £100 million a year. In addition, the dockyard has extended its remit to include yacht building. Over 3,000 local people now earn their income from marine leisure – little surprise when figures show that 30,000 from the area now take to the waters for recreational purposes. In addition, tens of millions of pounds have been invested in the Plymouth waterfront, thanks largely to the release of land formerly occupied by the Ministry of Defence. Other waterfront areas have been reclaimed for such prestigious projects as the National Marine Aquarium, a sea fisheries complex, a huge leisure park and a glass-making exhibition centre. The new Mount Batten Centre is one of the best sailing and watersports venues in the country, while Plymouth's wealth of modern marinas has pushed it into second place behind Southampton in that field.

Despite the fact that it is not a very large city – the current population is 260,000 – Plymouth has been the birthplace, or home, of an astonishing galaxy of well-known figures. For example, in the first half of the nineteenth century it attained a distinction in the world of art unmatched by any other town in Britain. Sir Joshua Reynolds (1723–92), born in Plympton, established an international reputation for his paintings, becoming the first President of the Royal Academy. He was followed by James Northcote (1746–1831), Samuel Prout (1788–1852), Benjamin Haydon (1786–1846) and Sir Charles Eastlake (1793–1865), all born within the confines of modern Plymouth. Another Plymptonian was Sir George Treby, Lord Chief Justice. Prior to this appointment, he was Lord Lieutenant of London and later made a High Court judge. Many other notable Plymothians made their mark during the twentieth century, in areas ranging from the Services to politics, the church, the world of entertainment and sport.

Quite a record for a city which started life as a mean fishing village only 750 years ago! And it's in keeping with this great city's achievements that forty-two other towns around the world have taken its name.

The Start of the Century

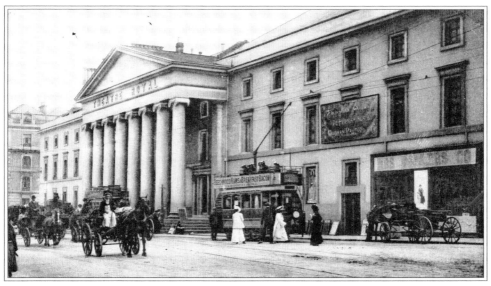

There is grace in this scene, with the majestic, pillared Theatre Royal, built in 1813, taking central role. A tram waits outside while a horse and waggon plod their weary way.

A favourite old-timer was the beautifully-proportioned RMS *Mauretania* which called in Plymouth Sound to land passengers and mail. Passengers reached London quicker by rail from Plymouth than by remaining on board until they docked at a port nearer to the capital.

The area around which Plymouth was founded. In the eleventh century, it was known as Sutone or 'South Farm'. At the time of the Norman Conquest the population was a mere seventy but, as the fishing and other trades grew, so did the number of inhabitants. By 1900, it was common to find 300 fishing boats in the harbour with a fleet of 70 trawlers averaging 34 tons each.

Regattas have always been popular events, from early medieval times. They drew huge numbers of spectators who, as here, often watched the proceedings while perched precariously in small craft or, more usually, from the grassy banks of the Hoe.

Sculling matches were extremely popular at the beginning of the twentieth century, although they were really glorified rowing-boat races. Water activities of all kinds have been second nature to successive generations of Plymothians, particularly those born on the Barbican. Mount Batten looms in the background – scene of bitter conflict during the Civil War in the seventeenth century.

Plymouth Argyle 1903-1904

Standing   W. ANDERSON   H. WINTERHOLDER   C. CLARK   F. FITCHETT   J. ROBINSON   A. CLARK   J. BANKS   J. PICKEN   B. JAC
Seated   T. CLEGHORN   B. DALYRYMPLE   W. LEECH   A. GOODHALL   J. PEDDIE   H. DIGWEED   F. BRETTELL

The Plymouth Argyle football team, always an enigmatic force, was born in a house at Argyle Terrace, Mutley – hence the name – one night in 1888. Their first competitive match as a professional team took place at Upton Park, West Ham's ground, on 1 September 1903, as members of the old Southern League. Argyle joined the former Third Division (South) in 1920 but went on to be promoted five times from that division to the Second. The average gate in the 1952/3 season was 23,345.

Pupils of St James-the-Less School, West Hoe, practising a dance in 1911. The school and its namesake church next door were destroyed by bombs in 1941. The church was rebuilt at Ham, one of the city's many council estates.

North Road School in 1911, eleven years after elementary schooling became the norm. To most pupils of that era, education emphasised the three Rs, copperplate writing and six of the best for errant behaviour.

Churches in the early 1900s, and well beyond, provided a focal point for a multitude of social activities, far more than now. This is *Trial by Jury*, enacted by the St Budeaux Baptist Choral Society in 1905. Many churches boasted drama and music groups and large choirs were quite the fashion. Participants didn't even have to attend Sunday services!

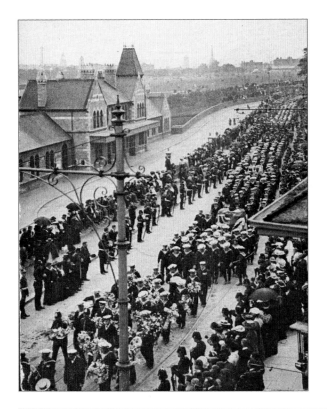

In 1905 the *A.8* submarine went down in Plymouth Sound at the start of her preliminary exercises. The crew of ten was lost and massive crowds turned out to pay their respects at their funerals. The procession is seen passing along Paradise Road. The London & South Western Railway station is on the left. Naval ratings, carrying wreaths, headed the solemn procession as it wound its way past the ancient Stoke Damerel church (below). This was an all too familiar sight in Plymouth which, as a major port, has known great grief through the centuries because of lives lost at sea.

Funeral Cortege of Victims of Submarine A passing Stoke Church.

The annual Good Friday 'bun fight', 1906. Customers gathered outside Perraton's, the bakery, in the Ridgeway, Plympton, from an early hour. The recipe for these special and immensely popular hot cross buns was a closely guarded secret. The bakery succeeded in drawing customers from far and wide to taste its succulent delights.

The Hoe has always been a splendid venue for events of all kinds. This Children's Day money-raising event took place in 1910, with proceeds going to a local homoeopathic hospital. Religious banners were never far away at an event of this kind (see far left).

Clearly, it wasn't a case of all work and no play when the National Union of Teachers conference came to Plymouth in 1910. This group of delegates, aided by local children, performed a curious-sounding musical called *Pixie Land*.

The northern end of Old Town Street, leading into Tavistock Road, 1911. The small boys, in their neat knickerbocker suits and stout, lace-up boots, pay little attention to the nearby traffic – but, then, there wasn't very much. The circular block on the left, not demolished until long after the Second World War, sported an illuminated clock above a motif which declared, 'Guinness is Good for You!'

The Theatre Royal, designed by the eminent architect John Foulston, opened in 1813 but, sadly, was demolished in 1936 to make way for a cinema, now the ABC. It had a seating capacity of just under 1,900, much the same as its modern counterpart which opened in 1982. The former Lloyds Bank building on the right, now a restaurant, is all that remains of the old George Street, which it partially fronted.

Regatta day, watched by thousands of people from the green slopes of Plymouth Hoe, 1910. This was always one of the most eagerly-awaited events in the city's lively social calendar. The Sound has always been an ideal venue for such events and the Hoe a splendid ampitheatre from which to watch them.

King George V's coronation was held in June 1911 and prompted celebrations all over the country. Plymouth has always risen to such occasions, so the large crowd on the Hoe was no surprise, and neither was the huge coronation bonfire to the left of Smeaton's lighthouse.

A closer view of the scene above. Part of the crowd is making its way to the western end of the Hoe, leading into Citadel Road, named for the large fortification erected there during the reign of Charles II.

As always, youth was to the fore in the festivities. These Boy Scouts really do seem to be enjoying themselves as, hats aloft, they produce the regulation three cheers for the new sovereign.

In another event to mark the coronation, schoolchildren enacted 'Old English May Day' celebrations, and very colourful it all must have been.

By night, Smeaton Tower on the Hoe was lit-up 'by electric lights', as a contemporary journalist helpfully explained. A searchlight swept the scene and fireworks followed.

Other parts of Plymouth celebrated the big day too. Decorations at Derry's Clock provided a central focal point. The clock was given to the town by Mayor Samuel Derry in 1833. It used to be called the 'Four-Faced Deceiver' because, so it was claimed, its four faces often provided four different times.

Devonport, created a separate borough in 1837, also held coronation festivities in 1911, as this huge bonfire in Devonport Park readily testifies. In 1914 the three towns of Plymouth, Stonehouse and Devonport were virtually forced to amalgamate into one borough.

The Alhambra Theatre, Devonport, enjoyed its heyday in the early 1900s. It was opened in Tavistock Street in the late nineteenth century by the rather unfortunately named Colonel Bastard and is the taller of the buildings in the distance. It was first known as the Empire and then the Metropole and its most successful productions were vaudeville. Stalls seats cost 2s 6d, pit 1s 3d, circle seats 2s, and gallery seats 5d. The theatre, by then a cinema, was blitzed in 1941.

Fore Street, seen here on 23 February 1910, was Devonport's principal shopping thoroughfare until the blitz of 1941, boasting many well-known household names, such as the local business of J.C. Tozer, draper's. Almost everyone in this area, and well beyond, had at least one family member working at the neighbouring dockyard which, from the middle of the eighteenth century, was the governing factor in Plymouth's economy. Part of Fore Street, together with its shattered buildings, was incorporated into the postwar dockyard extension.

Residents of Plympton, then outside Plymouth's boundaries, held a Lamb's Feast at Castle Green on 23 April 1911. Long before the Norman Conquest, there was a small community living on a mound where the castle now stands. Baldwin de Redvers quarrelled with King Stephen, who retaliated by sending in troops. The guard surrendered the castle which was then practically razed to the ground.

A garden fete in aid of St Mary the Virgin's organ restoration fund, Plympton, 1912. Enormous effort and imagination must have gone into the planning and execution of this Japanese tea garden theme.

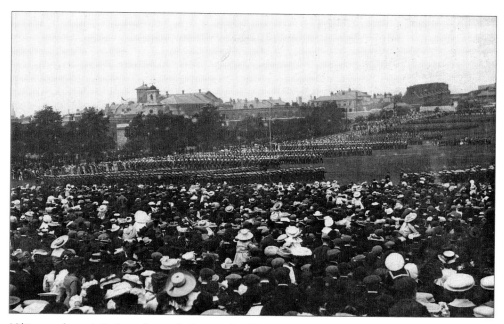

Military and naval displays often took place in the old garrison town when Plymouth had a large service population. This event took place at the Brickfields, Devonport, in 1912, scene of many a pageant and tattoo.

Plymouth was severely shaken by the *Titanic* disaster. The huge vessel was lost on 14 April 1912 after she struck an iceberg off Newfoundland. Over 1,500 passengers drowned out of 2,224. Some of the ship's crew who were rescued were brought to Millbay Docks and are seen looking over the rail of their tender as she draws in.

Many of the *Titanic*'s stewardesses were also saved. This group, again at Millbay Docks, had been fitted out with clothes by local ladies and stores. After a few days they were sent home, though several had to give evidence at the subsequent public inquiry into the disaster.

The Salvation Army built up an enormous following in Plymouth as a result of what it called its 'opening shots' in the 1870s, during which skirmishes with the local population were by no means unknown. The death of its founder, General William Booth, in 1912 was keenly felt, particularly since he had toured the area only the previous year. The memorial service at the Congress Hall, which seated over 2,000 people, was packed. Some of the mourners are seen here on their way to the event.

The residents of Stonehouse held a garden fete in the grounds of the sumptuous Winter Villa in 1912. This tableau oozes regality and patriotism. The building is now a residential home run by the Roman Catholic Sisters of Nazareth and is known as Nazareth House.

The deposed Empress Eugenie, former Empress of France, arrives at Millbay Docks off the steampship *Milwa* in 1912 to be received by a collection of local gentlefolk who showed her to her carriage – one of the early asylum seekers!

The Antarctic explorer Robert Falcon Scott was born and partly educated in Plymouth. The family home, Outlands, at Milehouse, was demolished and a church replaced it. The epic trek of his party to the South Pole in 1912, only to find the Norweigan explorer Amunsden had beaten them to it, has lived on in the annals of heroic exploits. Scott and his wife Kathleen are seen here in Cape Town, South Africa, awaiting the arrival of his ship the *Terra Nova* on her way south.

A party of Tibetans seeking refuge in a strange and foreign country, 1911. Understandably, they look jaded and dispirited after what must have been an exhausting journey. Many other groups of immigrants have arrived in Plymouth over the years, particularly from the West Indies.

Little did this happy group pictured in 1913 realise that just a year later the ship they were visiting, HMS *Carnarvon*, would be in a state of alert, ready to do battle with the German fleet. Visits to ships in port were immensely popular and were the forerunners of the modern Navy Days now held on a biennial basis.

Empire Day was taken very seriously during the period when Britain controlled half the world by fair means and foul. Many, but not all, schools gave their pupils a day off. But some of the boys were expected to spend part of this day helping in local events, such as this procession at the Recreation Ground in Saltash just over the River Tamar in 1910.

Here they are tramping behind a bugle-blowing band, sturdily marching up the main shopping street. Saltash has always been regarded as a dormitory town for Plymouth but has never lost a note of sturdy independence.

Sports day at the prestigious Plymouth College was a very well-organised affair, timed to perfection with immaculate displays of physical prowess. Many of Plymouth's leading lights have been educated at the college. This picture was taken at the 1910 event.

Regular 'dippers' off the Hoe were very common, many adopting bizarre club names. Here the Shackey Pool Stragglers and the Devon O'Clock Regulars strut their stuff in 1913, watched by admiring Mayor Sir Thomas Baker, the owner of the local Dingle's departmental store.

A new swimming-pool opened at Mount Wise in Devonport in 1913. The Mayor, Alderman Edward Blackall, is seen with Lord St Levan, on his right. He was Devonport's last mayor – the first, in 1837, was Lord Edward St Aubyn – because the borough was amalgamated with Stonehouse and Plymouth the following year at the behest of the Admiralty.

Plymouth's religious life has always been anything but predictable or routine. The Salvation Army made great strides after its stormy, action-packed arrival in the late 1870s, and the local commander, his wife and children were typical of many Salvationist families at that time.

The dark clouds of war burst on an unsuspecting and unprepared population in 1914. Many Plymouth families were to be decimated by horrendous losses on the Western Front and at sea. This curt card summonsed men to the colours. Patriotism was strong and the old adages still held sway. But not for long.

NATIONAL SERVICE.

18 — 61.

If **You** are **above** Military Age
You can **enrol** for **National Service!**
The Country calls for your help!!

DO IT NOW!

Full Particulars at

Grand Jury Room, Plymouth,

37 St. Aubyn Street, Devonport. } Committee Rooms.

or any Labour Exchange.

The 5th Devons were among the many regiments that set sail from Plymouth. The scene at Friary station was to be re-enacted again and again. In this case the destination was India, considered a 'soft touch' compared to France or Belgium. Some were fortunate enough to spend the entire war there.

Charity efforts for the war gathered pace at home. Regular, if unusual groups, bathed off the Hoe and this is one of them in action again at the Plymouth Swimmers' gala from which all the proceeds went to help blinded soldiers and sailors.

Empire Day, 1916. The boys of the Naval Brigade marched through Guildhall Square, passing the general post office *en route*. Presumably because of its vast service connections, Plymouth has always been adept at waving the flag with fervour.

Winston Churchill was an infrequent visitor to the area – until, that is, his son, Randolph, stood as an unsuccessful candidate for one of the local parliamentary seats in the 1950s. As First Lord of the Admiralty Churchill helped to shape naval strategy. This visit to the RN Barracks, Stonehouse, was in 1916.

Between the Wars

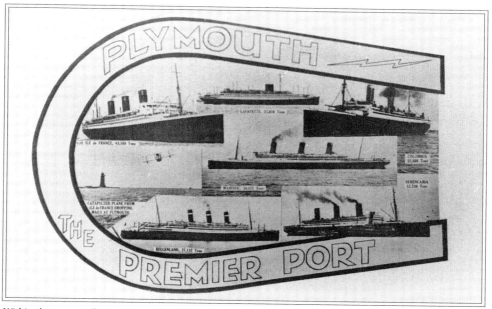

Within the magnet illustrated on this 1930 card are the *Ile de France, Columbus, Belgenland* and the *Berengaria*, just a few of the great liners that used to call regularly at Plymouth. So did such ocean thoroughbreds as the *Normandie, Bremen, Paris, Liberté* and even the great *Queen Mary*. Southampton gradually ousted its western neighbour from the passenger liner trade and jet air travel spelled the end for both terminals.

The Prince of Wales, later King Edward VIII, was much liked for his boyish charm and genial informality when he visited the West Country. He came to Plymouth in June 1919, to visit wounded servicemen. Contemporaries record that he talked to them at great length, and was able to sympathise with their plight. He was also told about what the corporation's plans were for postwar housing, given that Prime Minister Lloyd George had promised 'a land fit for heroes to live in'. The Mayor, Alderman J.P. Brown, showed him proposals for the North Prospect scheme, which became the city's most comprehensive housing project during the 1920s.

In 1919 Nancy, Lady Astor was elected to Parliament. She was to represent Plymouth Sutton for the next twenty-five years and was the first woman to take her seat in the Commons, where she soon made her mark. The by-election had been forced by the elevation to the Lords of her husband, Waldorf Astor, who had represented the constituency since 1910.

The scene at St Andrew's Church in 1919 when the memorial to American navalmen and the Door of Unity leading to the ancient Prysten House were unveiled. The cost was met by the Daughters of America. It all commemorated the close links Plymouth had established over the centuries with America.

Lady Astor receiving a key from building contractor Mr A.N. Coles to open the new maternity home in Durnford Street, Stonehouse, 1922. She officiated at hundreds of social and political events in Plymouth over the next twenty-three years. She died in 1964, aged eighty-five.

43

Many famous visitors arrived in Plymouth during the 1920s. In 1923 the bass soloist Sir Harry Lauder was greeted at the railway station by local worthies including, second right, Isaac Foot, who was beaten at the hustings in 1919 by Lady Astor. He was the doyen of a famous Plymouth family, which included Michael and Dingle Foot, and himself won the Bodmin seat for the Liberals in the 1920s. He was Plymouth's Lord Mayor soon after the Second World War.

The Prince of Wales, later Edward VIII, often visited the city. One of his engagements in 1923 was to inspect a company of local Girl Guides at the South Devon Hospital fair. Note that nearly all the gentlemen wore spats – a very comfortable article of clothing, popular until the 1950s and worn by some even now, including the author.

Jimmy Moses, a great character who was a stalwart in the local Labour Party, opened Plymouth's Civic Week in 1927, when he was the Mayor. A representation of Old Father Time, complete with scythe, the Carnival Queen perching on her throne and girls sporting the city crest on their dresses help to make this an evocative picture.

Jimmy Moses was Plymouth's first Labour Mayor and, later, MP. He was known as a 'people's friend' – in other words, something of a soft touch! He left school at fourteen to become an apprentice shipwright and in 1895 began thirty-four years of continuous service in the Dockyard. Jimmy was elected as Member of Parliament for Plymouth Drake in 1929, losing the seat two years later. At the 1945 general election, as a very sick 72-year-old, he was taken on a stretcher to cast his vote for his old colleague, Bert Medland who romped home at Drake.

The Queen of Romania, seen here at
Devonport in 1925, enjoyed a warm
rapport with the crowds wherever she
went. On this occasion she visited the
Alexandra Maternity Home at Stoke,
opposite Devonport Park. She was dressed
in a shimmering blue gown. Queen
Marie was the daughter of the Duke of
Edinburgh, former Commander-in-Chief at
Mount Wise, Devonport.

The GWR's *King George the Fifth* at Plymouth's North Road station after her first run with the prestigious Cornish Riviera Express in 1927. Until it was rebuilt in 1962, the station was little more than an unsightly collection of wooden shacks, hardly changed since it was first erected in 1877.

Plymouth Corporation trams and a pneumatic-tyred bus in 1925 at the Milehouse transport depot, opened in 1923. The final trams went out of service in 1945, but now there is talk of bringing back their modern counterparts. Many trams were open-topped so that you were assured of a thoroughly good drenching when it rained.

The Prince of Wales's brother, the suave, handsome Prince George, unveiled the impressive naval war memorial on Plymouth Hoe on 24 July 1924. It now carries the names of nearly 8,000 Plymouth-based sailors who lost their lives in the two world wars. There is an almost identical momument at Southsea Common.

Empire Day was eagerly anticipated by schoolboys of my generation. It signalled a half, or even whole, day off school, including at Mount House, my preparatory school. What was there to do? Oh, plenty of things, including, in 1937, inspecting the flying-boats gently rocking in the Sound.

The airship R100 passes silently and majestically over the naval war memorial on the Hoe in the summer of 1930. She was the sister ship of the ill-fated R101 which crashed in France with loss of life the following year.

Happier events also took place in 1930. The new bathing houses and terraces at Tinside, below the Hoe, were an enormous attraction to bathers and spectators alike, particularly as they were added to and refined in succeeding years. Tinside, added to in 1935, has been in a sad state of disrepair for some time, much to the anger of local people.

All kinds of facilities appeared in the early 1930s. The Mayor, Alderman Sir Clifford Tozer, gives a gentle push on a boy's yacht at the opening of a new pond at Central Park in 1931. Plans were announced in July 2000 for a multi-million redevelopment of a section of Central Park, to include a new stadium for Plymouth Argyle FC.

Communities were much more neighbour conscious in the '30s than they are now. Each area of Plymouth seemed to put on its own annual event, as here in Rendle Street in 1933. It was carnival week and everyone took a hand in making it a success. This was one of the poorer areas of Plymouth, but elderly people tell me that everyone was more content to take part in home-arranged events then.

Of course, the Services contributed greatly to the general aura of spectacle. Trooping the Colour was a 'must' for many, thrilled with the precision and smartness of it all – as nowadays, too. The ceremony took place every year, usually, as here in 1932, at the Royal Marine Barracks, Stonehouse, which had opened in 1781.

Intrepid flyer Jim Mollinson landed in Plymouth in 1933 on his return from crossing the Atlantic with his wife Amy Johnson. The deputy Lord Mayor, Alderman George Scoble, seems to be shouting himself hoarse during the welcome!

The Duke of Kent toured parts of the city in 1933. Well-wishers turned out to give him what seems to be a rather muted welcome (but who can tell?) as he inspected new council flats in Peel Street. The Duke was killed in a flying-boat crash in 1941, but his widow, the much-loved Duchess of Kent, continued to visit the city.

Leslie Hore-Belisha was the Liberal–National MP for Plymouth Devonport from 1923 to 1945, and he was well liked as an ebullient man-about-town. He is remembered, among other things, for Belisha beacons, which he brought to the country's streets, and for his rather ignominious spell at the War Office which ended in 1940 when Neville Chamberlain sacked him for failing to produce more tanks for France. Michael Foot defeated him in the 1945 general election. When the result was announced, Hore-Belisha stomped off in a rage, never to be seen in the locality again.

Former Labour and Natiuonal Government Prime Minister, Ramsey MacDonald's body is brought ashore at Plymouth from HMS *Apollo* in 1937. He died while on a speaking tour of Africa. HMS *Renown*, soon to be sunk in the coming war, rests in the background.

Time for another Service spectacular – this one was held to celebrate the coronation of King George VI in June 1937. To mark the coronation, school pupils in Plymouth received mugs bearing pictures of the new sovereign. I remember mine.

These visitors to one of the country's great battleships, HMS *Renown*, drink in all they are being told about the working of a triple turret during a Navy Day in 1936. This event, now held biennially, always attracts people from a very wide area, even from as far away as Birmingham.

The enormous Wesley Church in Ebrington Street was virtually destroyed by fire in 1937 – a harbinger of things to come during the Blitz, which followed four years later. The congregation decided to join the nearby Central Hall, also Methodist, producing a typical Sunday morning and evening congregation of nearly 1,000. What remained of the gutted building was used as a Selleck's restaurant during and shortly after the war.

Roborough airport, on a former polo field, was opened in 1930. This picture, taken seven years later, shows Captain Phillips being presented with a cup after winning the Devon air race from Haldon to Exeter to Plymouth. The Lord Lieutenant of Devon, Earl Fortescue, is doing the honours watched by the Mayor, Walter Littleton.

Somewhere in Texas? No, somewhere near Plymouth! This was an incident (or should it be accident?) at the Dartmoor Rodeo at Yelverton, a few miles outside the city. Perhaps the would-be rider of a wild Dartmoor pony got more than he bargained for.

Earl Haig has been vilified by the media in recent years as a backroom butcher who needlessly sent millions of men to their deaths on the Western Front in the First World War. His widow, Viscountess Haig, took a keen interest in ex-servicemen (as he had done) and sometimes came to Plymouth in the course of her work. Efford Colony was a home in which some of the more badly wounded were cared for.

A harbinger of things to come, indeed! But these cheerful-looking women, complete with hair-curlers, had little idea, perhaps, of how soon they would be donning these gas masks for real. Meanwhile, they giggled away as they tried some for size at the 1938 Navy Week.

There was great excitement, of course, when Cunard's flagship, the *Queen Mary*, made one of her rare visits, anchoring off Cawsand Bay, in Plymouth Sound in 1937. As with similar ships, people waited at Millbay Docks to meet the incoming tenders in the hope of seeing famous Hollywood film stars – they often did.

Plymouth's main importance still lay in her huge naval dockyard. As the home port for many ships of the line, she played host to a vast number of sailors. The Senior Service responded by arranging many superb displays, such as this impressive turnout by the Home Fleet in 1938. A 'full house' was assured.

59

Families were much more stable and 'together' in the 1930s. Divorce was rare and socially unacceptable – though no one knew, of course, what went on behind the lace curtains. This Plymouth family from Compton, photographed in the mid-1930s, seem to exude contentment. The wife's hair-style and pince-nez, perched on her nose, were *de rigueur* at that time. So was her husband's starched collar.

Traffic in Plymouth before the war was very congested. This photograph was taken in 1938 at St Andrew's Cross with Spooner's Corner on the left. Old Town Street ran across the top with Henry Lawry's, ironmonger's, just visible. The city buses sported a fetching maroon and cream decor.

'Farley's Rusks . . . Baby Loves Them' – the advertisement is on a locally registered lorry heading towards Mumford's Garage, below the YMCA at the bottom of Old Town Street, next to Balkwill's, the chemist's, in the mid-1930s.

The inauguration of a new service from Roborough airport to Cardiff, 1932. In addition to such flights, people were keen on 15-minute 'flips' over the city. I remember being taken on one in the late 1930s in a twin-engined Andromeda. The pilot, probably ex-First World War, sported a neat brown beard and looked bored.

Tram No. 74, rebuilt from a Devonport Brill car. The ruck and electrical equipment was all new, however. These were sleek vehicles but made an enormous clatter and got in the way of the increasing number of private vehicles. The trams were constructed between 1918 and 1922.

Well, why not have a bit of fun? It was often reflected in the postcards in the 1930s, of which this is one example. This jolly gent, in his white spats, kicks his bowler into the air with gay abandon. Quite a guy!

The Zig-Zags were one of a large number of amateur singing groups who toured the Three Towns providing all-round entertainment. They had to be good; there was lots of competition.

The musicians called themselves the Frivols (short for frivolous?) and wherever they went they took a pet dog – probably he was the star of the show. This group sang straight stuff and was much in demand in pubs and clubs.

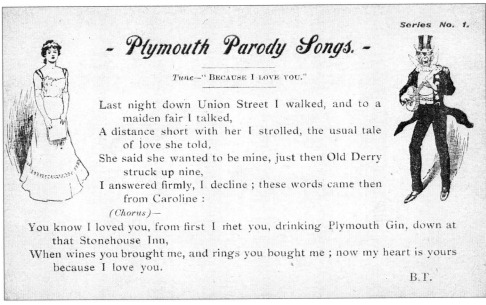

'Last Night down Union Street I walked and to a Maiden Fair I talked . . .' One of the many parody songs loved by former generations, all of them with a strong local flavour, just for the 'natives'.

'The latest news from Plymouth', no less, ending with that timeless phrase: 'Wish you were here!'

The Second World War and Beyond

It had to come. All the efforts to appease Herr Hitler had failed and 3 September 1939 saw the outbreak of the Second World War. It was a Sunday but that didn't stop the *Western Evening Herald*, as it was then known, from rushing out a special edition. A distraught-looking newsvendor is busily selling it, watched by a policeman with a curiously detached look on his face.

One of the most popular moves in wartime Plymouth was the election of Lord and Lady Astor as the city's leading citizens. Nancy Astor, in particular, was an immense tonic in helping to lift people's spirits during the Blitz. She and her husband, Waldorf, toured the areas wrecked by bombs, doing all they could to assist those left homeless and destitute.

One of the most inpiring events of the war was the return to her home port of the cruiser HMS *Exeter* (built in the Dockyard ten years previously) after her epic part in helping to put the mighty German battleship, *Graf Spee* out of action. She limped into port, badly battered, on 13 February 1940 and she was greeted by excited crowds.

Winston Churchill, as First Lord of the Admiralty, came down to congratulate the officers and ship's company, speaking to them on the quarter deck. Standing beneath the 8-inch gun are Captain Bell and the First Sea Lord, Admiral Sir Dudley Pound.

After France fell in June 1940, Germany had aerodromes from which it could bomb south-western England and this it proceeded to do with great ferocity. The worst raids over Plymouth were in March 1941 when vast tracts of the city were almost obliterated. This is one such scene.

'Your homes are down but your hearts are high.' That's what Winston Churchill said when he visited blitz-blasted Plymouth in April 1941 in the wake of the worst bombings they city had endured. Churchill wept when he saw the scenes of devastation. Not everyone was pleased to see him. 'Why don't you give it to 'em back?' was shouted from the crowds.

69

The Duchess of Kent, Princess Marina, with her unaffected charm and stunning beauty, was another welcome wartime visitor. The matron of the Royal Naval Hospital, Miss D.W. Beale, curtsies as she is presented during one such visit. Looking on is Admiral Sir Martin E. Dunbar-Nasmith, Commander-in-Chief, Plymouth.

By 1944, when the raids stopped, nearly 5,000 buildings had been destoyed, including the Guildhall, the library, many churches, buildings of historic importance and hospitals. In addition, nearly 71,000 buildings had been badly damaged, 1,174 civilians killed and 3,269 seriously injured. This picture shows George Street in 1943.

A view of Old Town Street, its shopping centre no more. The circular block at the top survived the war but was demolished in the 1970s to make way for a precinct and new roads.

Two years after the end of the war Plymouth was still a scene of appalling desolation as this 1947 shot shows. And many of the buildings that did remain were empty shells.

Devonport with its massive dockyard, had been a prime target for German raids. It lost virtually its entire shopping centre. Just two badly damaged stores still stood, Marks & Spencer and Burton's, but these were eventually enveloped by the dockyard extensions.

The scale of damage in the heart of Devonport is clear here. Little remained after the the Luftwaffe's visits. Unfortunately, Devonport was largely overlooked in postwar reconstruction, Plymouth receiving prime attention.

Planners argued that as Plymouth was the commercial hub of the entire city, rebuilding work should be concentrated there. The wreckage of Bedford Street, and the east side of George Street, seemed to reinforce that view. The pillared building is the remains of George Street Baptist Church, one of the great pre-war preaching centres.

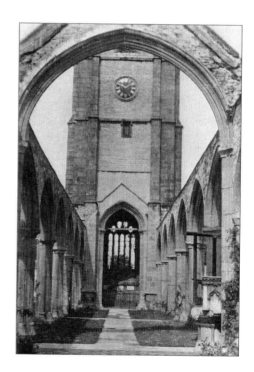

Nearby, St Andrew's Church was open to the skies, remaining so for many years. It was 1949 before the long and careful reconstruction began, and 1957 before it was completed. Her Majesty Queen Elizabeth II visited the church in 1977 during her Silver Jubilee tour.

Some slices of the old thoroughfares did escape total obliteration, including this stretch of the former Westwell Street which contained many household names, such as Churchill's, the fishmonger's, and the Jewel corner shop. A lovely little park and an ancient cemetery lay on the left of these shops, but were removed when reconstruction got under way.

March 1947 and the very first act in rebuilding Plymouth's shattered city centre was captured on camera. These workmen wielded their picks and up came part of Raleigh Lane, first instalment of the Royal Parade to be.

It would be many years before there would be anything close to the number of new shops needed to satisfy demand. Meanwhile, many traders moved into these small, cramped and sometimes damp Nissen huts which sprang up all over the centre as temporary refuges.

Reconstruction began in March 1947 with the cutting of the main east–west shopping street, Royal Parade. In October, King George VI and Queen Elizabeth came down to inaugurate the work. It was a festive occasion. I was there with my first real 'sweetheart', Betty Lovell, and I remember it well. Here, the royal visitors line up with the civic party before proceeding to the podium. On their right is the Lord Mayor, Alderman Sir Harry Taylor, who, ironically, was one of the few councillors opposed the bold Abercrombie-Watson 1943 plan for reconstructing Plymouth.

The royal couple were greeted in 1947 by flag-waving schoolchildren as they continued their walk down the partly finished Royal Parade. It was a gay day indeed, and a harbinger of good things to come.

In 1948 there were physical signs of the city centre's rebirth with the laying of Royal Parade at the junction with the former Westwell Street.

A few months later, and this is how it looked. The building in the centre is the sandstone-covered Prudential Assurance which had to be demolished to make way for a new thoroughfare. Many people missed its silent dignity.

Royal Parade flanked by Nissen huts and bombed sites. The reconstruction plan included three parallel shopping streets with an impressive north–south avenue cutting across them, and it was realised.

Almost all of the heart of Plymouth was gutted, even as late as 1949. Rebuilding was under way but many of the scars were to remain for a long time.

Several years on and the gaps are filling up, though much remained to be done. But many of the large stores were open by the time this picture was taken in 1952, though the gigantic Co-operative Society building, at the foot of the picture, was still being rebuilt. It is now called Derry's.

A close-up of some of the larger stores in Royal Parade. Spooner's, in the foreground, was an old family firm later taken over by the Debenhams chain, as was its near-neighbour, John Yeo's. Shoppers greeted these gleaming new arrivals with great relish.

Reconstruction under way in Old Town Street, February 1951. Steel structures, with armies of men swarming all over them, were a common sight in those years. And seeing this tangible evidence of our city's physical rebirth gave a great lift to all our spirits!

The 1943 futuristic Watson-Abercrombie plan for Plymouth – as intended. Shame it didn't work out quite that way. Shortage of cash, miserly steel allocations, and so on, meant that the great plan had to be trimmed down, some would say dumbed down. So, the scheme for a large forecourt, tree-lined boulevards and a hotel near the railway station didn't materialise.

Old Town Street, rebuilt, looking south from Royal Parade in 1954. The pillared building was the Norwich Union offices, with shops underneath, and Boot's was the next block.

Lady Astor could still cut a dash in 1952, when she was well into old age. She was always an activist. She had her enemies, of course (Winston Churchill among them), but most people would agree that she was by far the most charismatic MP Plymouth has ever known.

The Queen Mother visited the city in 1953, just a year after her daughter's coronation. She was feted lavishly, and the warmth she exuded to the crowds was reciprocated. Here she is accompanied by the Lord Mayor, Harry Wright.

The coronation of Queen Elizabeth II in June 1953 was celebrated with great joy in Plymouth, as elsewhere. Street parties were all the rage. This one, in Victory Street, Keyham, was typical.

Field Marshal Lord Montgmery, victor of El Alamein, came to open the rebuilt Guildhall in 1959. The decision to rebuild had been passed by the City Council by just one vote! Flanking him are the Lord and Lady Mayoress, Mr and Mrs Percy Washbourn.

Prince Philip, Duke of Edinburgh, has been to Plymouth many times. He did part of his naval training at HMS *Britannia*, Dartmouth, not far away. He is seen here walking down Royal Parade in July 1958 accompanied by the Lord Mayor, Alderman George Wingett, and his wife, the Lady Mayoress. Behind her is Stanley Green, a doyen of the local photographers, who caught city events on camera over many decades. Two of the city's newer buildings are in the background.

Winston Churchill did his best to see his son, Randolph, home and dry at the 1951 General Election, here speaking on his behalf in the grounds of Saltram House. But the old magic didn't work, and Michael Foot again took the seat, Plymouth Devonport, for Labour. Randolph was anything but exuberant throughout the campaign; he knew he was a 'goner' almost from the start.

In 1959 Lady Astor received the freedom of the city she had served so well – and not before time, many thought. She smiled her way through the packed Guildhall, with Lord Mayor, Percy Washbourn, a Devonport butcher by trade, on her left. The old lady was wearing well!

The 1960s and '70s

The 1970s Eastlake Walk shopping precinct, offically opened by Princess Anne, seemed splendidly surreal when it was new, but it has since grown tatty and unkempt. It is to be replaced by a large shopping mall, thus reviving the eastern end of the shopping centre.

In 1961 the Queen Mother paid a visit to the Devonport-based *Ark Royal*. She was greeted off her plane by the Commander-in-Chief, Plymouth, Vice-Admiral Sir Charles Madden. Her Majesty had just turned 81, and probably didn't anticipate hitting her 100th birthday so many decades later!

The commander of the *Ark Royal*, Captain P.J. Hill-Norton escorts Her Majesty along the flight deck. Later that day, she inspected the Royal Marines Guard of Honour in the hangar. This was followed by further inspections and then a march past on this, the *Ark Royal*'s third commission.

Queen Elizabeth II officially opened the new civic centre on 25 July 1962. It took four years to build at a cost of £1.7 million and dominates the city's skyline. Large crowds welcomed the 36-year-old monarch. Only yards from here is the flagstaff which her father, King George VI had unveiled in 1947. The Queen was accompanied by her husband.

The civic party walked with the Queen as she made her way to the new civic centre colossus. With her is the Lord Mayor, Alderman Harry Mason, one of the forces in the postwar rebuilding. His wife, the Lady Mayoress, accompanies the Duke of Edinburgh.

Plymouth Argyle in their 1964/5 Second Division season at Home Park. Their new manager, Malcolm Allison is squatting beside them. Left to right, back row: Duncan Beale, Johnny Williams, Dave Maclaren, Doug Baird, Reg Wyatt, Frank Lord. Front row: Dave Roberts, Cliff Jackson, Dave Corbett, Johnny Newman (Captain), Mike Trebilcock, Nicky Jennings, Bill Cobb.

As council house estates proliferated, so did the seemingly insatiable demands for facilities of all kinds. Many tenants were young couples and nursery schools had to be provided for their families. This one served one of the earliest and largest estates at Whitleigh on the northern flanks of the city.

Plymouth did not escape the phenomenon of the Beatles! Screaming fans sometimes drowned out the sound of their music and they certainly took the city (or its younger element) by storm. Some fans went wild in an escatic frenzy. Teens and twenties queued all night to obtain tickets to see their musical idols, letting off yelps and screams as soon as the band came on stage. Looking back, these same people may now wonder what all the fuss was about!

Do you remember these fashions of the '70s? Perhaps you wore them. These youngsters, streaming under the North Cross subway, don't actually look too different from today's . . . or do they?

Mayflower 70 Celebration lasted for five months and marked the 350th anniversary of the voyage of the Pilgrim Fathers to America. Concerts, bowls in period costume on the Hoe (where else?), madrigals, painting and craft exhibitions, cycle races, tennis tournaments, pageants, an air show, carnivals and a religious service all celebrated the voyage.

Many churches were rebuilt in the decades after the war on new housing estates or in the inner suburbs. Catherine Street Baptist Church opted for a modern-style building in the city centre. This was the successor of the George Street Baptist Chapel, which was destroyed in the Blitz. It could trace its roots right back to before 1620, when its congregation entertained the Pilgrim Fathers on their way to the New World.

The Christian Community Church developed a new building at Shaftesbury Villas, on the northern fringes of the city centre. This is one of many new, or 'house', churches which have been built in Plymouth, many composed of dissidents from the mainstream denominations.

95

It may not be beauitful but it was needed. The bus station for long-distance and intermediate coach and bus services opened in the 1970s, putting an end to the unsatisfactory position of having departure points scattered all over the city. Charles Church, built in the 1640s and behind the bus station has been preserved as a memorial to Blitz victims.

The pannier market was a blaze of colour and put the flags out to celebrate the Queen's Silver Jubilee in 1977. Her Majesty paid a visit to the city that year and it was claimed that she was genuinely surprised by the warmth of her welcome. The market, at the western end of New George Street and Cornwall Street, was significantly upgraded in 2000. It needed to be.

To the End of the Century

The north–south axis of Armada Way links Plymouth railway station with the Hoe. Many old buildings were demolished to make way for this thoroughfare.

Princess Margaret opened the new Theatre Royal in 1982. There had been a desperate need for such a facility for decades, given that so many theatres and cinemas had gone in the war. Only the stately old 1898 Palace remained and this had been turned over to other uses.

Now acclaimed as one of Britain's top provincial theatres, the Royal presents a year-round programme of top class entertainment, from ballet, opera and contemporary dance, to musicals, comedy drama and pantomime. It hosts regular visits from the Birmingham Royal Ballet and the Glyndebourne Touring Opera, and is now the fourth 'home' of the Royal Shakespeare Company. And to think that one city councillor forecast it would be the West Country's biggest 'white elephant'.

The Barbican, Plymouth's Elizabethan area which escaped destruction in the war, has been gently revived and beautified over the years. It is now a pleasing blend of old and new, and it is the city's main tourist area.

The mood in Plymouth during the 1982 Falklands War was sombre. Plymouth soldiers were among those serving and city-based troops were in the thick of the fighting. Military bases in Plymouth were on full alert with convoys passing constantly through the city, which also dispatched many navy ships, including the carriers HMS *Hermes* and HMS *Invincible*. This picture shows Royal Marines disarming Argentine soldiers on Stanley airfield.

People lined the old quaysides as one group of men after another of returned from the Falklands. Some placards even carried the first names of some of them. Such crowds probably gathered for the first time to greet Sir Francis Drake after he had helped defeat the Spanish Armada in 1588.

101

When it was all over, there was a great atmosphere of relief and exuberance. Jubilant crowds turned out to greet the servicemen home again. This one lined Royal Parade. The fourteen-storey civic centre looms in the background.

Prime Minister Margaret Thatcher was at the peak of her popularity during and immediately after the Falklands War. So, she was sure of a gutsy wlecome when she toured Plymouth. Here she shows members of the public notes she had taken from that famous handbag of hers – the one she used to thump at Council of Europe meetings.

Ken Headon had something to shout about in the 1980s – he was Plymouth Town Crier. Ken's remit was to promote Plymouth's tourist industry – very loudly. He even went to Houston, Texas, to promote the city.

Christmas decorations in Plymouth city centre during the 1980s. The first picture shows the heart of the shopping area, marked by the sun-dial. (Surely they could have thought of something more impressive?) This stands at the junction of New George Street and Armada Way. Thousands of people from a wide area nightly pack into Plymouth during the prolonged, and often frenetic, Christmas shopping season.

103

'Can't pay: Won't pay.'
We all remember this
communal war-cry directed
against the hated Poll Tax.
The tax triggered mass
protests in Plymouth, as
elsewhere. This mainly
good-humoured crowd
milled around the city
centre, banners aloft, on its
way to the Hoe in 1988.

105

Princess Diana glittered and glowed in all directions as she met her admirers. You can see the rapture on their faces as the Princess chats with a group on a visit to the city in the 1980s.

(*Opposite*) Opening Day, Plymouth Dome, March 1989. The queues stretched along Madeira Road at the foot of the Hoe. Modern technology has established the Dome in Britain's premier league of heritage attractions. Patrons can experience the voyages and encounters that helped shape the world, walk amid the stench and grime of an Elizabethan street, operate a ship's radar and TV camera to scan and enlarge ships on shoreline, and, as they say, much, much more.

Dingle's smouldering. No, not as a result of enemy bombing but thanks to animal rights protestors who objected to the store selling fur. It was 1988 and the protesters caused £13.2-million worth of damage. The fire began at 10 p.m. and ripped through the upper floors. Over 100 firemen tackled the blaze which lit up the sky 'just like the blitz' and explosions showered debris into the streets below.

A few churches are still expanding in Plymouth, for example the Methodist Central Hall which, in 1997, held a service of thanksgiving for a new restaurant-cum-outreach area called the Discovery Centre. Seated, left to right, in the front row, are the Minister of that time, the Revd David King, the chairman of the Plymouth and Exeter District, the Revd Kenneth Hext, guest speaker the Revd Martyn Atkins from Cliff College and the former Minister and his wife, the Revd Geoff and Mrs Jean Sharp.

The catalyst for the Barbican's regeneration programme was the harbour company's decision to construct a lock at the entrance to the former tidal harbour, and to build a new fisheries complex and deep water quays, partly on reclaimed land, opposite the old Victorian fish market on the Barbican, opened in 1995. This, in turn, was redeveloped to house the Barbican Glassoworks.

The Services have always tried to identify with the civilian population of the city which hosts them. Former Rear-Admiral Peter Daunt opened this pre-school at Crownhill in 1994 – with help from the children, of course.

Cyber cafés began to spring up in the late 1990s, and they are certainly here to stay. Clients part with a mere £1 in order to surf on the Internet. Young people are the keenest customers, a large number of whom trawl through the Net to try to land a job – or a girlfriend.

109

Princess Anne frequently visits the West Country, often to inspect the Services, with which she has many links, and at other times to monitor the many good causes of which she is patron. She is seen here in Saltash in 1998: she was shown a number of enterprises to help disabled and disadvantaged people.

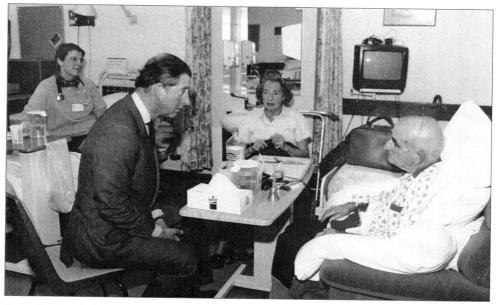

Prince Charles talked to virtually every patient when he visited St Luke's Hospice in January 1999. His genuine empathy was remarked upon by many of the patients and staff.

The prince had a number of engagements that day, including this visit to Montpelier Junior School, where he seemed to be entranced as the little ones showed him their computers with an easy nonchalance.

The world-class National Marine Aquarium opened in 1998 is a tremendous boost to the city's tourist industry. It is an important centre for marine education, conservation and research as well as being a leading aquarium. Highlights include a huge deep reef tank, a coral reef and a shark theatre. This is its wider setting, near the historic Sutton Pool and the Barbican, with a cluster of new and old developments around it.

The massive Barbican Leisure Park includes a multiplex cinema, bars, restaurants, night clubs, ten-pin bowling, a fitness centre and more besides. And it was all built in 1998 at downtown Coxside on the site of an old gasworks.

The Queen paid a flying visit to Plymouth in June, 1999, (She must know the city pretty well by now!). On this occasion she visited a high-tec factory and a school, among other places. In spite of a brisk itinerary, the indomitable old lady showed no signs of wilting. The gentleman behind her, to the left, was Devonport MP David Jamieson.

Owned by a consortium of its berth-holders, the Mayflower International Marina completed in the 1970s is close to the mouth of the River Tamar. It is completely self-contained and is accessible at all states of the tide. The Marina has been awarded the industry's highest 'Five Gold Anchor' accolade and is one of several now at Plymouth.

The northern edge of the city centre. The railway station mini-skyscraper is at the top, right-hand corner, with the University of Plymouth complex ahead, on the far side of the road between the two roundabouts.

The eastern end of Royal Parade. The large, squat building in the foreground, next to the ABC cinema, is a multi-storey car park. The Civic Centre looms large over the landscape, faced by the large department stores fronting Royal Parade. The Theatre Royal stands at the end of Royal Parade, almost cheek-by-jowel with another car park.

A low aerial shot of the centre, with the gleaming department stores in their full glory. Dingle's was the first to open, in 1951, and people queued all night to be the first to savour its delights.

The beautifully proportioned Duke of Cornwall Hotel escaped damage during the Blitz and stands as a monument to much that was good in Plymouth's pre-war architecture. It opened in 1863, mainly to cater for passenger traffic from Millbay railway station, almost opposite, which was then an important terminus.

The Tamar Bridge was considerd a modern marvel when it opened in 1962, linking Plymouth by road with south-east Cornwall. In 2000 it had to be strengthened and widened.

Acknowledgements

My thanks are due to Westcountry Publications, owners of the *Evening Herald* and *Western Morning News*, for the loan of many of their file pictures, without which this book could not have been compiled so comprehensively. It was my privilege to serve on the reporting staffs of those two newspapers as a local government correspondent and feature writer for nearly twenty years.

HM Dockyard, the source of so much craftsmanship and resources for the Royal Navy for over 300 years. In spite of cut-backs, it remains the largest naval base in Western Europe.